SWEDEN

DENMARK

BRUNSWICK

BRANDENBURG

POLAND

Germany

Wittenberg

SAXONY

HESSE

Cracow

NZ

HOLY
ROMAN EMPIRE

TZERLAND

Terraferma

MILAN

Vicenza
Padua VENICE

Pavia
Lodi

O T T O M A N

MANTUA   FERRARA

Parma

Bologna

GENOA

Forlì

Rimini

FLORENCE

Urbino

River Arno

PAPAL
STATES

SIENA

River Tiber

Italy

Rome

E M P I R E

NAPLES

Greece

E A

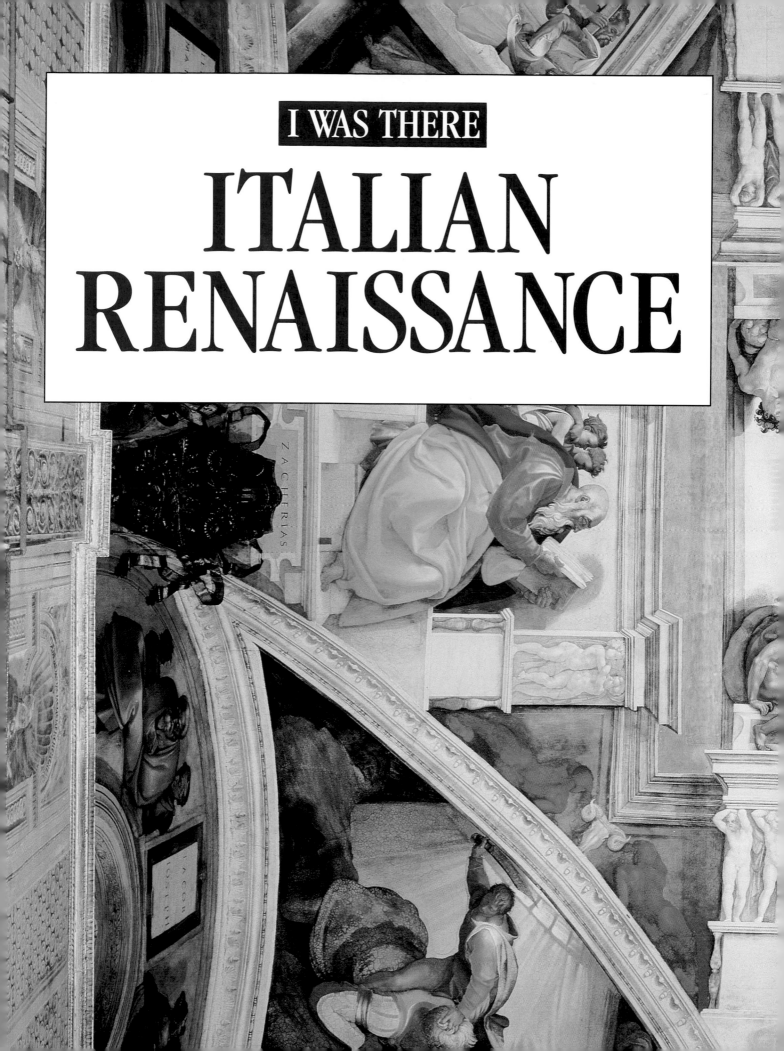

I WAS THERE

ITALIAN RENAISSANCE

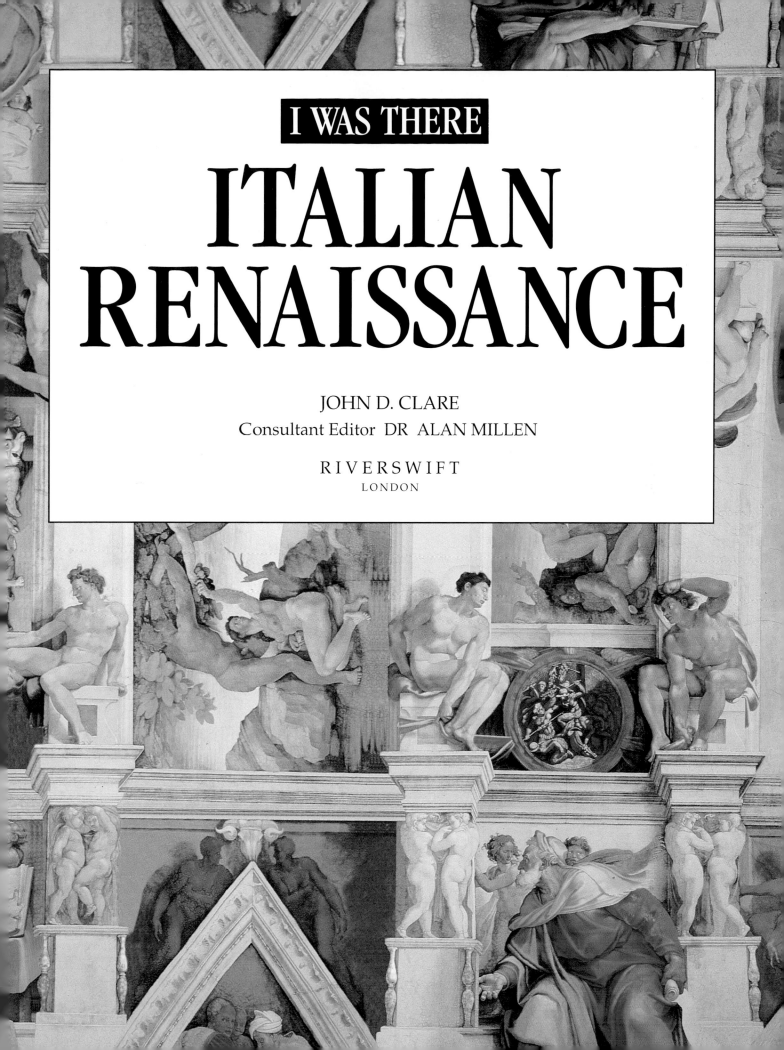

I WAS THERE

ITALIAN RENAISSANCE

JOHN D. CLARE

Consultant Editor DR ALAN MILLEN

RIVERSWIFT

LONDON

First published in Great Britain in 1994
by Riverswift, Random House,
20 Vauxhall Bridge Road, London SW1V 2SA

Random House Australia (Pty) Limited
20 Alfred Street, Sydney, NSW 2061, Australia

Random House New Zealand Limited
18 Poland Road, Glenfield, Auckland 10, New Zealand

Random House South Africa (Pty) Limited
PO Box 337, Bergvlei 2012, South Africa

ISBN 1-898304-00-9

A CIP catalogue record for this book is available from
the British Library.

Photography Charles Best
Director Tymn Lintell
Production Manager, Photography Fiona Nicholson
Costume Designer Val Metheringham
Set Design and Props Cluny South
Make-up Designer Emma Scott
Designer Dalia Hartman
Visualizer Antony Parks
Series Editor Helen Wire
Editor Gilly Abrahams
Map and time-line John Laing
Map and time-line illustrations David Wire
Typeset in 11/14 Palatino Dalia Hartman
Reproduction HBM Print Pte Ltd, Singapore

Printed and bound in China

ACKNOWLEDGEMENTS
Casting: Piccolo Teatro, Siena; Teatro Comunale di Firenze.
Fresco consultant: Faith Vincent. History consultant: Richard
Mackenney. Jacket concept: Peter Bennett. Location consultants:
Alta Macadam and Sammie Daniels. Location finders: William
Larson and Antony Parks. Photography assistant: Michael
Harvey. Transport: Peter Knight, Road Runner Film Services.

Riverswift would also like to thank:
Tim Angel, Libby Clohisey and Denny Edwards of Angels
and Bermans; Philippa Devon, Rita Smith and Stephen
Francis of the BBC Wig Department; Dottore Lapo
Bramanti; M.J. Hughes and Roy Randall, University of
Cambridge; Gary Bevans, Frank Burns, Michael Lambert
and Fr. Enda Naughton of the English Martyrs Catholic
Church, Goring-by-Sea; Aldo Marinelli and Gianfranco
Natali of Antonio Frilli, Ltd; Italian State Tourist Board;
Keeley Hire; Michael's Coins; Nippon Television; Dottore
Patrizio Osticresi, Opera di Santa Maria del Fiore; Oreste
Pelagatti; Baron and Baroness Ricasoli; Monsignore Angelo
Livi, Chiesa de San Lorenzo; and Angi Woodcock.

Additional photographs: Ancient Art & Architecture
Collection: p17 top; p24 bottom. Ashmolean Museum,
Oxford: pp36-37. Biblioteca Medicea Laurenziana, Florence:
p46 bottom. Bibliothèque de l'Institut de France, Paris:
p41 middle left. Bridgeman Art Library, London: Christie's
London pp54-55; Museo Real Academia de Bellas Artes,
Madrid pp58-59; British Library p63 bottom right. British
Library: p62 bottom right. A.F. Kirsting: p10 top. National
Gallery, London: (detail) pp32-33; (detail) p40 top right.
Nippon Television Network Corporation, Tokyo 1991:
(details) p1, pp2-3, pp4-5. Antony Parks: front cover, Urbino;
pp44-45. Royal Collection: p23 top right; p38 middle left.
Scala, Florence: p6; p7 (2); p9 (2); (detail) pp12-13; p13 top;
p14 bottom right; pp18-19 (4); (detail of head by Fra
Angelico) p21; p22; p23 bottom; p26 middle left; (detail)
pp26-27; p27 bottom right; p31 top; p33 top; (detail)
pp40-41; p44 (2); p45; p48 top; (detail) p48-49; (detail)
pp52-53; p62 top. The Wellcome Institute Library, London: p60.

Contents

The End of the Middle Ages

The world in 1400 was completely different to today. In Europe, the King of England ruled large parts of France, the Muslim Moors ruled Granada in southern Spain, and south-eastern Europe was part of the powerful Ottoman Empire. Italy and Germany were collections of small independent states (although the Holy Roman Emperor was nominally the overlord of Germany and northern Italy). The pope claimed to be the spiritual ruler of all of Christendom, yet he was also the ruler of a small, rebellious state in central Italy.

The richest area of Europe was northern Italy, particularly the city-states of Florence and Venice. Both were republics (not ruled by a king). Venice controlled a small empire in the Mediterranean. Europeans did not yet know that America existed, and refused to believe the descriptions the Venetian merchant Marco Polo (1254–1324) had given of his visit to China.

Above all, the people of the Middle Ages had a different system of beliefs from those of today. For medieval people, the terrors of the unseen - hell and demons - were as real as the brutal world of famine, disease and massacre

in which they lived. It was believed, for instance, that all children in the English village of Strood were born with tails (as God's punishment to the inhabitants for once pelting Saint Austin with fish tails). When a visitor found that not one of the children was deformed in this way, he did not doubt the story but merely blessed the mercy of God.

The idea that there had been a 'Renaissance period' became popular after 1860, when the Swiss historian Jacob Burckhardt published his book, *The Civilization of the Renaissance in Italy*. The French word *renaissance* means rebirth. Writers of the late nineteenth century used it to describe 'the change from the Middle Ages to the Modern World', which they said took place between 1400 and 1600. To them, this period was when mankind rediscovered the classical world (ancient Greece and the Roman Empire) and the civilization of Italy blossomed; it was, wrote the English historian J.A. Symonds, the time when 'humanity awoke as it were from slumber and began to live'.

People living at the time of the Renaissance certainly thought that something new was happening. The term 'the Middle Ages' was invented by the Italian scholar Flavio Biondo (1392–1463) to describe the period of stagnation between the glories of Rome and the achievements of his own period. Fifteenth-century writers described their period as the 'new age' in which a 'renaissance' of learning had revived a lost 'ancient elegance'.

Was there a Renaissance?

Some modern historians do not accept that there was a Renaissance in the years between 1400 and 1600, because they think the idea is based on an unfairly negative view of the Middle Ages. According to Symonds, for instance, medieval people were 'semi-barbarous…pathetic…[living] amidst stupidity and ignorance…devoted by superstition to saints and by sorcery to the devil'. No wonder he decided that the Renaissance was 'the liberation of humanity from a dungeon'.

During the sixteenth century the period

immediately before the Renaissance was labelled the 'Gothic' period; it was said to have been as barbaric as the Goths who had destroyed the Roman Empire. Nowadays, historians are more ready to accept that the Middle Ages had scholars, artists and architects of genius. Medieval Gothic architecture, with its towering interiors and narrow stained-glass windows, is awesome. The Gothic style of medieval art used differences in the brightness of the paint, and overlapping figures of different sizes, to give the illusion of

depth. According to one music historian, medieval rhythms were not equalled until the 1950s. If we think medieval people were 'stupid', it is because we have failed to understand their outlook and attitudes.

Yet, if the Middle Ages were not a time of stupidity and decay, how could there have been a rebirth of learning during the Renaissance? Some historians have argued that the years 1400–1600 merely marked the 'flowering of the Middle Ages'. Others have portrayed

the period as the beginning of the Reformation (a time of changes in religion, c. 1500–1700).

Nevertheless, most modern historians agree that there was a period or movement we can call the Renaissance, although they all choose different dates. During the fifteenth century (sometimes called the Classical Renaissance) there was a conscious attempt to change the whole of society - politics, the arts and literature, learning, manners and religion - to imitate the Greeks and the Romans (see pages 8–31). It is perhaps the only time that historians have shaped the course of history!

Later, during the High Renaissance, the emphasis moved to the discovery of new knowledge and ideas (see pages 40–53). Individuals such as Leonardo da Vinci (1452–1519), Michelangelo (1475–1564) and Raphael (1483–1520) extended the boundaries of human achievement. It was, writes the modern historian J.H. Plumb, 'an age...of violence that threw up geniuses with the ease of a juggler'.

This book will consider some of the changes that took place during the Renaissance, and you will be able to decide for yourself whether this period was the beginning of the Modern Age.

Far left: in the Middle Ages, people are forced to accept what they are told. In this medieval painting, a heretic (someone who does not believe the Church's teaching) is burned to death.

Examples of Gothic art and architecture: left, Christ's entry into Jerusalem, by Duccio (c. 1260–1318); below, Gloucester Cathedral in England.

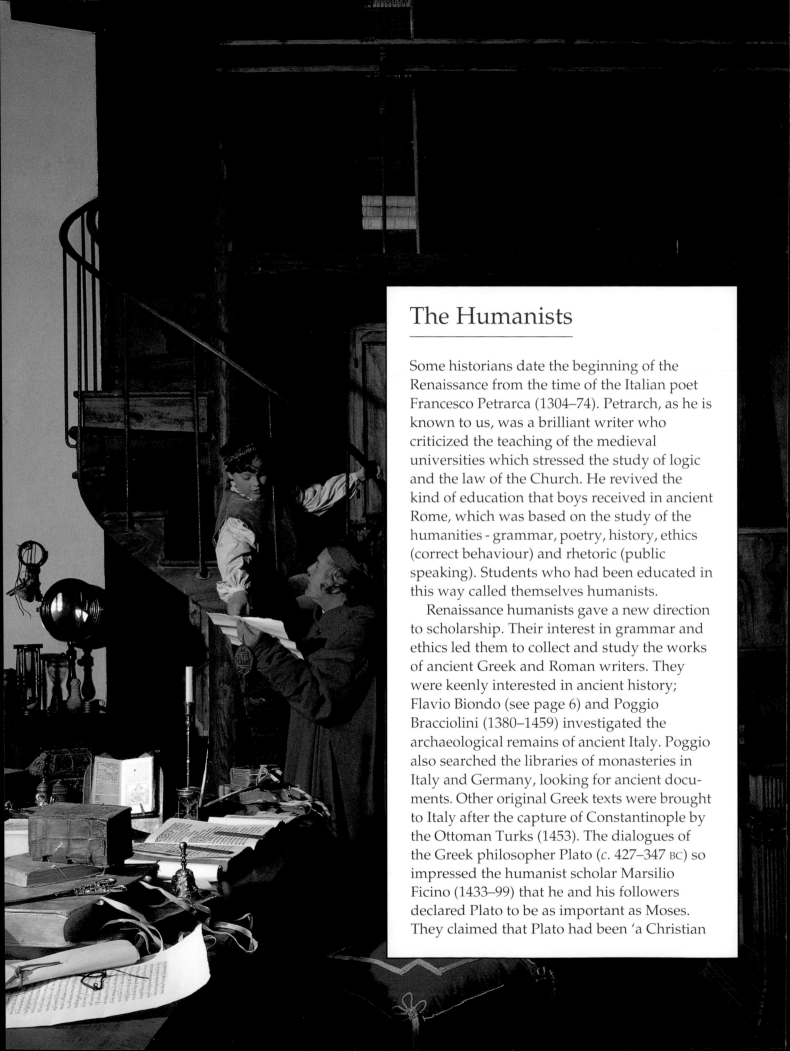

The Humanists

Some historians date the beginning of the Renaissance from the time of the Italian poet Francesco Petrarca (1304–74). Petrarch, as he is known to us, was a brilliant writer who criticized the teaching of the medieval universities which stressed the study of logic and the law of the Church. He revived the kind of education that boys received in ancient Rome, which was based on the study of the humanities - grammar, poetry, history, ethics (correct behaviour) and rhetoric (public speaking). Students who had been educated in this way called themselves humanists.

Renaissance humanists gave a new direction to scholarship. Their interest in grammar and ethics led them to collect and study the works of ancient Greek and Roman writers. They were keenly interested in ancient history; Flavio Biondo (see page 6) and Poggio Bracciolini (1380–1459) investigated the archaeological remains of ancient Italy. Poggio also searched the libraries of monasteries in Italy and Germany, looking for ancient documents. Other original Greek texts were brought to Italy after the capture of Constantinople by the Ottoman Turks (1453). The dialogues of the Greek philosopher Plato (*c.* 427–347 BC) so impressed the humanist scholar Marsilio Ficino (1433–99) that he and his followers declared Plato to be as important as Moses. They claimed that Plato had been 'a Christian

troublemakers with dangerous new ideas. Lorenzo Valla (1407–57), for instance, wrote an influential textbook on the Latin language. However, he also criticized the existing Latin translation of the Bible, and when he proved that *The Donation of Constantine* (a document giving the pope the right to rule central Italy) was a forgery, the pope was furious.

Main picture: many humanists are employed as tutors for the children of Italian rulers and nobles.

Above left: *The Birth of Venus* **by the Florentine painter Sandro Botticelli (1444–1510) is influenced by the writings of Plato. It shows Venus (representing love, beauty and the human race) being reborn out of the formless sea, just as civilization is being reborn after the chaos of the Middle Ages.**

Below: four of Florence's humanists, painted by Domenico Ghirlandaio (1449–94). They are said to be Ficino, the Latin scholar and poet Cristoforo Landino, the poet Politian, and Demetrios Chalkondylas, the professor of Greek at the academy in Florence.

before Christ'. The neo-platonists (new Platonists) and their ideas - that beauty and love were revelations of God - were very influential during the Renaissance.

Above all, Renaissance humanists believed in 'the genius of man…the unique and extraordinary ability of the human mind', as praised by Gianozzo Manetti (1396–1459) in his book, *The Dignity and Excellence of Man*.

Humanists became teachers, lawyers and politicians. They criticized other scholars as out-of-date and even barbarous. In contrast, they described themselves as 'universal men', with a broad knowledge of all subjects. To emphasize their modern outlook, many humanists adopted a new *italic* style of hand-writing (which they mistakenly thought was used in classical times) instead of the medieval Gothic script. It is this humanist propaganda that has led, in part, to the belief that the Renaissance was a time when civilization and learning advanced.

The first humanists were regarded as

Florentine Civic Pride

In 1402 a chance event occurred which ensured the success of humanism in the republican city-state of Florence.

For 12 years the city had been at war with Gian Galeazzo Visconti, the Duke of Milan. The Chancellor of Florence during those years was the humanist scholar Coluccio Salutati (1331–1406). In a series of brilliant propaganda articles against Visconti he portrayed Florence as a new Roman republic, fighting for freedom against tyranny. Gian Galeazzo admitted that Salutati's pen did more damage than the Florentine cavalry!

In 1402, with his armies in control of the surrounding cities and ready to attack Florence, Gian Galeazzo fell ill and died. Florence had survived and the struggle had convinced the Florentines that republicanism and humanism were right. As one historian has written: 'To become aware of one's ideals, there is nothing like fighting for them.'

Humanist ideas were enthusiastically adopted by the nobles and wealthy merchants of the city. Humanists were appointed as city officials and teachers. In 1427 the Florentines appointed the humanist scholar Leonardo Bruni (1370–1444) as Chancellor. Bruni's book,

In Praise of the City of Florence, claimed that Renaissance humanism had originated there.

'Florence is the home of the cleverest people. Whatever they do, they do it better than other men, be it warfare, politics, study, philosophy or trade,' writes Bruni. 'Civic' humanism develops in Florence; the idea that it is each citizen's duty to act for the common good. Pride in their city leads Florentines to fund building projects and to commission works of art.

In 1401 the sculptor Lorenzo Ghiberti (1378–1455) wins a competition to design and make the bronze panels for the north doors of the Baptistry building (above). They take him 21 years to complete. Soon after, he is asked to make the east doors; these take him a further 27 years (main picture), but are said by Michelangelo to be 'worthy of the gates of paradise'.

Wealth and Patronage

In the fifteenth century Florence was one of the richest states in Europe. The Florentine gold coin (the florin) was used as currency all over Europe.

The wealth of Florence was based on its 21 *arti* (guilds). These were associations of craftsmen or merchants which had strict rules designed to maintain high standards of work. The wealthiest was the *Arte di Calimala* (the guild of cloth merchants). At the peak of the city's prosperity, Florentine merchants produced every year seventy thousand pieces of fine material dyed in brilliant yellows and reds; each was stamped with the seal of the *arte* as a guarantee of its quality. They sold them throughout Europe. There were six other major *arti*: the wool merchants, silk weavers, bankers, lawyers, spice merchants and fur traders. The members of these guilds were nicknamed the 'fat people'.

More than one hundred thousand people lived in Florence. The vast majority were poor. There were never more than six thousand members of the 21 guilds and most of these people were small craftsmen (the 'thin people') who had little money to spare. The cultural achievements of the period were paid for, therefore, by a tiny number of very wealthy rulers and merchants. Their wealth provided the patronage (financial support) for most of the works of art produced during the Renaissance.

Why did the ruling class spend so much money on patronizing the arts?

Civic duty was a major influence. The *Calimala*, for instance, accepted responsibility for the upkeep of the Baptistry building, and it was they who employed Ghiberti in 1401 (see page 10). Florence cathedral was the responsibility of the wool guild; they commissioned the architect Filippo Brunelleschi (1377–1446) to build the cathedral's dome (see page 17).

The Church taught that it was evil to make money by trading or lending money, so many merchants felt sinful and tried to earn God's forgiveness by public patronage. The wealthy Florentine merchant and banker Cosimo de' Medici (1389–1464) poured money into the building of churches; he spent more than forty thousand florins on rebuilding the convent of San Marco in Florence.

Books and things of beauty also gave a wealthy patron an opportunity to escape from the violence and suffering of everyday life. Cosimo built for himself Roman-style villas in the countryside and had them decorated with

frescoes and statues. His grandson Lorenzo the Magnificent (1449–92), who had been educated by humanist teachers, said that learning provided relaxation at those times 'when my mind is disturbed by the tumult of public affairs'.

Patronizing the arts was one of the ways in which rich people (especially rulers, see page 26) could flaunt their wealth. Cosimo de' Medici founded a Platonic Academy in Florence and supported humanist scholars such as Ficino. Lorenzo collected Greek and Roman antiquities and invited humanists and artists to discuss philosophy at his table. He spent more than half his income on books and, according to one writer of the time, it was Lorenzo who revived the writing of literature in the Italian language instead of in Latin.

Public patronage was also the way important men demonstrated their political power. Perhaps this explains why they commissioned busts and equestrian statues (see page 18) of themselves. Lorenzo the Magnificent poured money into festivals and tournaments, employing a host of artists to make the masks, banners and floats. Musicians were also needed for these events, although Lorenzo himself wrote some of the songs for his carnivals. His extravagance helped to cause the collapse of the family's banking business in 1490. The Medici family had dominated Florence since 1434, and the result of the bank's decline was a financial and political crisis which permanently damaged the city's economy.

Main picture: artists often include in their paintings the patrons who commission their work. Amongst the wise men in *The Procession of the Magi*, the painter Benozzo Gozzoli (1420–97) includes the young Lorenzo de' Medici (below, on a white horse). Following him, also on horseback, are his father Piero and his grandfather Cosimo.

Top: the Medici's Villa di Castello, near Florence.

The main currency used by traders is a coin that contains 3.5 grams of gold. Depending on its place of origin, this is called a ducat (from Venice, right) or florin (from Florence).

Painting in Perspective

A major problem for painters was how to depict three-dimensional scenes from life on a two-dimensional (flat) surface. Sometime after 1410, the architect Filippo Brunelleschi discovered that artists could make their paintings more realistic than medieval art by using what he called perspective.

Brunelleschi had noticed that the parallel stripes of green marble on the angled sides of the Baptistry in Florence seemed to get closer together the further away they were. He developed a system of mathematical perspective, whereby an artist could convincingly recreate this effect on a flat surface to give the illusion of distance. Brunelleschi's ideas became

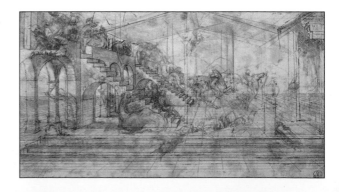

well known after they were published by the architect Leon Battista Alberti (1404–72) in his book, *On Painting*.

One of the first artists to use the new technique of perspective was the Florentine painter Masaccio (Tommaso di Giovanni, 1401–28), who broke away from the Gothic style of painting (see page 7). The most enthusiastic student of the new ideas, however, was another Florentine painter, Paolo Uccello (1397–1475). According to legend, when his wife suggested he came to bed, he said he preferred to stay with his 'sweet mistress, perspective'.

Left: the theory of perspective, illustrated in Leonardo da Vinci's sketch (*c.* 1481) for the background of a painting of *The Adoration of the Magi*. The artist has imagined a 'vanishing point' on the horizon (behind the rearing horse in the centre). All the lines of the drawing are then projected back to this single point. In this way the scene seems to have three dimensions. Like many of Leonardo's projects, the painting is never finished.

Main picture: an artist uses a screen, known as Alberti's veil, to get the correct perspective for his drawing of the lute. He has drawn a grid to correspond to the veil, and now he copies what he sees, square by square. To give the illusion of depth he shortens the lines projecting away from the onlooker; this technique is known as foreshortening.

Architecture

Classical Greek and Roman buildings (see page 8) fascinated Renaissance humanists such as Flavio Biondo and Poggio Bracciolini. Many buildings had survived from ancient Roman times (for instance the Pantheon and the Colosseum in Rome) and they were copied by Renaissance architects.

Filippo Brunelleschi, who was asked to design the dome of Florence Cathedral in 1418, had never before built a dome. He had, however, carefully studied ancient Roman buildings, even to the point of climbing onto the roofs and taking off the tiles. He had also read the books written by the Roman architect Vitruvius. It took Brunelleschi over 16 years to build the dome, which became a model for all future domed buildings.

Brunelleschi's buildings used other classical design features recommended by Vitruvius (see main picture). The art historian Giorgio Vasari (1511–74) believed that Brunelleschi had been 'sent by heaven to give architecture new forms, after it had wandered astray for many centuries'.

Later Renaissance architects introduced more changes. When Donato Bramante (c. 1444–1514) redesigned the Tempietto (little temple) of San Pietro in Rome for Pope Alexander VI, he broke away from the

cross-shaped plan of medieval churches and followed the circular plan of a typical Roman temple. Other Renaissance architects revived Vitruvius's ideas about town planning. They proposed that towns should be designed like Roman cities, with sewers, aqueducts and a strict mathematical grid of streets and spacious squares - although few of their schemes ever came to anything.

Main picture: many architects copy the features of the church of San Lorenzo in Florence, designed by Brunelleschi. His design follows classical principles; it is based on the circle and the square, and the different parts of the building are proportioned according to mathematical ratios (notably 1:2:5). He also uses Greek-style Corinthian columns.

Above: the Temple of Neptune at Paestum, an ancient Greek colony in southern Italy, is one of many buildings which have survived from classical times.

Sculpture

Like the architects, Renaissance sculptors tried to imitate classical forms. The Florentine sculptor Donatello (Donato Bardi, 1386–1466), who had been Ghiberti's pupil, went to Rome to study the remains of classical statues. Between 1416 and 1435 he carved a number of statues for the bell tower of Florence Cathedral; the most famous, nicknamed *Zuccone* (pumpkin-head), looks exactly like a Roman senator in his toga.

As in classical times, Renaissance sculptors made equestrian monuments (statues of men on horseback) and busts of famous people. In 1443 the city of Padua commissioned Donatello to make a bronze statue of one of their military leaders, Erasmo da Narni, who was nicknamed Gattamelata (Honey-cat). Donatello portrayed him on horseback, in classical armour, like a Roman general. Donatello's pupil Andrea del Verrocchio (1436–88) made a number of busts of leading Florentines, including both Cosimo and Lorenzo de' Medici, and in the year of his death finished a 'flawless' equestrian statue of the Venetian general Bartolomeo Colleoni.

Verrocchio was typical of many of the artists of the Classical Renaissance. One of the most influential artists of his time, he worked in his

bottega (workshop), helped by his assistants and apprentices, producing for the Florentine merchants and nobles a range of works of art including pictures, chairs, statues, plates and goblets, and even a ceremonial suit of armour. He was not wealthy; his tax return for 1457 claimed that he was not earning enough to be able to buy hose (stockings) for his workers. Like the medieval artists and stonemasons, he was primarily a craftsman. Only later in the Renaissance did artists achieve fame and high social standing (see page 29).

Far left: the Roman statue of Emperor Marcus Aurelius (the only equestrian statue which has survived from ancient times) provides an example for both Donatello's statue of Gattamelata (below left) and Verrocchio's statue of Colleoni (below). Such statues reflect the importance of imitation of classical forms, and the Renaissance emphasis on the individual.

   Right: reviving a common form from ancient times, Donatello's *David*, cast in bronze (*c*. 1430) for Cosimo de' Medici, is the first life-size nude figure of the Renaissance. Donatello is the son of a wool-comber; when Cosimo gives him a red cloak (a rich man's garment) he declines to wear it.

A Painter at Work

Fresco, a method of painting known since Roman times, was particularly liked by Renaissance artists. Cennino Cennini, author of the *Craftsman's Handbook* (1390), described it as 'the sweetest, most attractive way of working there is'. Making a fresco involves painting directly onto a newly plastered wall with a mixture of pure pigment and lime water. As the artist works, lime in the wet plaster mixes with the paint and reacts with the carbon dioxide in the air, forming a hard, permanent surface. The colours this technique produces seem translucent (shining).

Considerable skill is involved. The artist has to complete the work before the plaster dries (the Italian word *fresco* means fresh). A mistake can be put right only by waiting until the plaster dries, chipping it off and starting again.

High up on scaffolding, the Renaissance artist would be dealing with the difficult parts of the painting while his apprentices brought more paint or worked on less complicated sections. More than once, artists were said to have fallen to their death in the confusion.

Because blue pigment turns green when combined with lime, the sky was usually added *a secco* (when the plaster was dry). Paint applied to dry plaster, however, often peeled off later.

Below, top left: the first step when painting a fresco is to plaster the wall. Sometimes artists cover the wall with matting made from woven, flattened cane, in an attempt to stop damp coming through later. Two layers of plaster are applied to the wall to give a thick, flat, absorbent base for the fresco. Onto this the artist will sketch a rough design in a browny red pigment. The sketch, called a *sinopia*, gives the patron an idea of what the finished fresco will look like.

Opposite, below left: when the artist is ready, an apprentice makes the paints. This highly skilled task involves grinding together metal oxides, minerals such as ochre, and many other substances such as berries, flowers, and insects (until the fifteenth century, artists are members of the same guild as doctors and chemists). Meanwhile, another workman puts a thin top layer of plaster over a patch of wall (the *giornata*). Because the paint must be applied to the plaster while it is wet, he covers only as much of the wall or ceiling as the artist can paint in a single day (*giornata* means a day's work, roughly six to eight hours). The size of the *giornata* varies, therefore, according to how much detail the artist has to paint in that particular section of the fresco.

Opposite, top right: most artists prepare cartoons (drawings on paper) in their studios, and set their apprentices to prick hundreds of tiny holes round the outlines of the drawing. Before they start painting, they place the cartoon over the wet plaster. A muslin bag containing pigment is pressed against the holes in the cartoon; the pigment goes through onto the wet plaster. When the artist joins the dots (opposite, below right) he gives himself an outline to follow when he paints the fresco.

Main picture: the artist paints quickly from top to bottom of the *giornata*. Details such as buttons and jewellery are added when the fresco has dried.

Advances in Art

Renaissance artists developed three types of paintings: portraits, landscapes and still-lifes. Breaking away from the medieval custom of painting mainly religious scenes, they began to paint scenes from history and from Greek and Roman myths. One historian has calculated that, whereas in the 1420s only one-twentieth of all paintings were of a secular (non-religious) nature, by the 1520s one in five had a secular subject.

Above all, there was a change in the atmosphere of the paintings of the Renaissance. Artists were excited by the new ideas and techniques they had discovered; they felt, as Alberti wrote, that 'man can do all things if he will'. A typical Renaissance 'universal man' - architect, poet, playwright, mathematician and athlete - Alberti had good reason to feel that way. 'You have been given a body more graceful than other animals…sharp and delicate senses…intelligence, reason and memory like an immortal god,' he wrote. Consequently, Renaissance painters filled their paintings with nude figures of beautiful women and handsome, muscular men. They also paid more attention to the setting in which their subjects were placed, filling even their religious paintings with people, pets, possessions, plants, buildings and landscapes. Where Gothic paintings had been solemn, majestic and often sad, the people in many Renaissance paintings seem to be enjoying life.

Artists also made a number of technical

developments during the fifteenth century. For instance, they started to use oil paint. Before the Renaissance they had used tempera (powdered pigments mixed to a paste with egg yolk). A number of paintings by Leonardo da Vinci were ruined because he experimented with new kinds of paint (see page 38).

Andrea Mantegna (1431–1506) is one of the most important artists of the Classical Renaissance.

Left: his *Parnassus* (1497) is a typical Renaissance painting of a classical myth, taking delight in the human body, the fierce landscape and the background details. Venus, the goddess of love, and Mars, the god of war, embrace while the nine Muses dance and sing, causing volcanic eruptions. To the left are Vulcan in his forge and Orpheus playing a lyre. On the right stand Mercury and the winged horse Pegasus, who stamps his hoof to stop the eruptions.

Below: in a fresco painted on the ceiling of the Camera degli Sposi in the Palazzo Ducale in Mantua (c. 1473), Mantegna uses the technique of foreshortening (see page 15).

Above: Mantegna is one of the first artists to try to make the details of his paintings historically correct, as in, for example, *Trumpeters, Bearers of Standards and Banners*, one of a series of paintings called *The Triumphs of Caesar* (c. 1480–95).

Books and Printing

The Renaissance began many years before the first printed books, but one modern historian has stated that without printing there could not have been a Renaissance.

Before printing, every book had to be copied by hand onto calf-skin parchment. In about 1439, however, a citizen of Mainz in Germany called Johann Gutenberg (*c.* 1399–1468) invented a press which allowed printing to be done mechanically. For some years craftsmen had been experimenting with blocks of wood onto which the text of the book was carved. Gutenberg developed the idea of moveable metal letters which could be assembled in any order to form the text.

The first printing presses in Italy were set up during the 1460s. At first, people did not like the look of the new printed books, so printers left spaces for scribes to add decorations by hand. Wealthy patrons even employed scribes to make hand-written copies of books that had been printed!

By 1500, however, there were more than two hundred printing presses in Venice alone, and the Venetian printer Aldus Manutius (1449–1515) was producing large numbers of classical Greek and Roman texts in pocket-sized editions - the Aldine classics. Aldus established the importance of a clear, accurate, easy-to-read text.

Printing allowed the Renaissance to spread, first to all the Italian states (see page 26), and then to the rest of Europe (see page 60). Because books could be produced more cheaply, scholars could study the texts more easily. This made the new ideas available to a wider audience. Moreover, as books became easily obtainable, men and women who wished to appear cultured had to be well read.

Mechanical printing: the letters are assembled in a forme (frame) and inked with an inkball (top left). A sheet of paper is placed over the forme and a workman pulls the lever of the printing press to press the paper onto the type (main picture). In this way the text is printed on the paper (centre left).
Left: the Gutenberg Bible, printed in 1455.

The Courts of Italy

Soon, Renaissance culture began to spread from Florence to other Italian states. Many of these states were not republics; they were ruled by 'princes' - kings, dukes, marquises and counts. These rulers, who vied with each other to look cultured, modern and better than the rulers of other states, employed the best artists and writers of the time.

This patronage was vital to the spread of the Renaissance. According to the Florentine historian Francesco Guicciardini (1483–1540), Italy's 'most brilliant reputation among all other nations' was due to the fact that 'Italy was not only rich in population, trade and wealth…she was full of noble minds learned in every branch of study and art'. The 'noble minds' of men such as Leonardo da Vinci, however, could never have flourished if Italy had not also been 'blessed to the highest degree by the magnificence of many princes'. It was this mixture of wealth and talent which created the Renaissance.

Naples

In Naples, King Alfonso I (who ruled from 1442 to 1458) read the books of the Roman authors Livy and Seneca every day. He spent the vast sum of twenty thousand ducats a year supporting humanist scholars such as Lorenzo Valla (see page 9). He especially favoured the historian Bartolomeo Fazia, who wrote a flattering biography of him.

Alfonso's son Ferrante I (ruled 1458–94) built up a large library of Italian poetry and supported the *Accademia Pontaniana*, a group of scholars, led by the humanist Giovanni Pontano, who met to discuss poetry.

Milan

In Milan the ruling Sforza family supported humanist writers and had their children educated by humanist teachers. During the time of Duke Lodovico Sforza (ruled 1494–1500) and his wife, Beatrice d'Este, Milan became a centre for the study of Greek and Latin. According to Beatrice's secretary, 'the court was full of men of every skill and talent, especially poets and musicians, and no month passed without some production or play'. One of the artists employed at the court was Leonardo da Vinci.

Ferrara, Mantua and Rimini

In the tiny duchy of Ferrara, the Este family were patrons of the Renaissance. Leonello d'Este (ruled 1441–50) commissioned buildings by the architect Alberti, and frescoes by the artist Mantegna. Under Duke Ercole d'Este (ruled 1471–1505), Ferrara became a centre of poetry and drama. The poet Lodovico Ariosto (1474–1533) was employed there as a diplomat. His influential poem *Orlando Furioso* (Mad Roland) celebrated the Este family, comparing them to the heroes of ancient legends.

In nearby Mantua, Gianfrancesco Gonzaga (ruled 1407–44) invited the great humanist teacher Vittorino da Feltre (1378–1446) to set up a school for the children of the nobility. Vittorino believed that school ought to be enjoyable; he called his school 'the Pleasant House'. He also accepted girls, and admitted a few children from poor families who did not have to pay. Gianfrancesco's son Lodovico (ruled 1444–78) was educated at Vittorino's school. A keen humanist, he always carried a copy of

Caesar's *Gallic Wars* on his military campaigns; he also employed Alberti and Mantegna. Under Francesco II (ruled 1484–1519), who was married to Isabella d'Este, the court became a centre of the Renaissance, famous particularly for its musicians. Isabella longed to have her portrait painted by Leonardo da Vinci (who had painted her sister), but he never produced more than an unflattering charcoal sketch.

The ruler of the papal territory of Rimini, Sigismondo Malatesta (ruled 1432–68), employed humanists to write poems celebrating his military successes as well as his love for his wife Isotta. He also commissioned Alberti to redesign the church of San Francesco in Rimini in the style of a classical temple. Known as the Tempio Malatestiano, it is richly decorated with sculptures of pagan gods, signs of the zodiac, the Malatesta coat of arms and the magnificent tombs of Sigismondo and Isotta.

Urbino

Remarkably, one of the major centres of the Renaissance was the tiny duchy of Urbino. In the mountains of central Italy, Urbino was one of the states which owed allegiance to the pope. It was less than 40 miles (64 kilometres) square, but it developed into perhaps the most refined of all the Renaissance courts.

Duke Federico da Montefeltro (ruled 1444–82) was educated at Vittorino's school in Mantua. He seems to have been the model of a cultured Renaissance prince. According to his librarian and biographer, the duke was very religious; he attended Mass twice a day, and forbade swearing and gambling at court. He maintained a household of five hundred people, including four humanist teachers, five architects, five engineers, four transcribers of manuscripts, and five readers who, during meals, read aloud the works of Livy.

Duke Federico employed the architect Francesco Laurana (*c.* 1430–1502) 'to make our

city of Urbino a beautiful residence worthy of…our own status', and spent a fortune on the arts, bringing painters and tapestry-makers from Flanders. His library - on which he spent thirty thousand ducats - contained copies of all the Greek, Latin and Hebrew texts then known, books on church history and theology and a complete series of Italian poets, as well as books on mathematics, music, military tactics and the arts. In times of scarcity, he bought grain for the poor, and lent money to shopkeepers who had got into difficulties. 'I am not a merchant. It is enough to have saved my people from hunger,' he is said to have commented.

Below: Federico da Montefeltro with his son, Guidobaldo. Federico continues to have books copied by hand long after printing is commonplace; each volume is bound in red leather embossed with silver.
Left: the family of Lodovico Gonzaga of Mantua, a fresco (1472) by Mantegna in the Camera degli Sposi.

The Courtier

The court at Urbino, as it was in 1506, was idealized by the writer Baldassare Castiglione (1478–1529) in his book *The Courtier*. By this time, Duke Federico had been succeeded by his son Guidobaldo (ruled 1482–1508). According to Castiglione, the young duke possessed 'as well as a friendly and charming nature, an infinite range of knowledge'. His wife, Elisabetta Gonzaga from Mantua, had such modesty and nobility that 'those seeing her for the first time realized that she was a very great lady'. Around them gathered a large group of courtiers (members of the inner circle of the duke's friends); they were all 'very noble and worthy gentlemen…poets, musicians, buffoons of all kinds, and the finest talent of every description anywhere in Italy'. Amongst them was the painter Giovanni Santi (Raphael's father) and of course, Castiglione himself, who stayed in Urbino from 1505 to 1508.

Days at the court of Urbino, said Castiglione, were spent in 'honourable and pleasing activities of the body and the mind', such as tournaments, riding, games and musical performances. At night the ladies and gentlemen of the court amused themselves by taking part in intellectual debates.

The Courtier describes a series of these discussions. These have given us our picture of the perfect Renaissance man, for one of the topics was: 'What makes the ideal courtier?'

It is the year 1506, in Urbino, Italy. Talking long into the night, the guests outline the attributes of the perfect courtier. He must be a 'universal man'. Culture, grace and refinement, noble birth, courage on the battlefield and sporting ability are vital. He must be educated and able to speak well. He should show a knowledge of the classics and be able to understand art and sculpture. Singing and dancing are essential skills. He must eat politely, without making noises by grinding or sucking his teeth. He must be witty; even practical jokes are acceptable, but it is important not to go too far. A great deal of time is spent discussing servants and clothes; a man with very fat or very thin legs should not draw attention to them by wearing brightly coloured hose. The good courtier must be modest and should make his achievements seem effortless, but at the same time he must make sure that his virtues are seen. Finally, he must be unquestioningly loyal to his prince.

The women who attend the debates are as keen as the men to express their opinions. Two poets, two musicians and a sculptor take part in the discussions, alongside the courtiers, state officials, soldiers and visiting nobles. Forty years ago (in the time of Verrocchio, see page 19), most artists had come from the craftsman class. By the time of *The Courtier*, they have risen in status and are accepted into the upper classes of society.

Renaissance Women

One of the topics which the courtiers at Urbino addressed in their discussions was the proper place of women. According to Castiglione, one of the men, Ottaviano Fregoso, openly declared women to be 'very imperfect creatures, of little or no dignity compared with men, and incapable in themselves of performing any good act'. This was a commonly held opinion in Renaissance times, although there was no doubt that the women at the court of Urbino were not inferior; the discussions were led by the duchess Elisabetta and her friend Emilia Pia. One night, at a nod from the duchess, the ladies of the court playfully attacked one of the male guests who had become too anti-feminist.

Nevertheless, some writers have argued that during the Renaissance the social position of most women remained inferior. Young girls were often kept shut up in the home or in convents. At a marriageable age - sometimes as young as eight or ten years old - they were 'sold', on their father's instructions, to a suitable man who would make a good ally for the family. 'Entry forbidden to geese, women and goats,' read the sign at the gate of a public garden in Florence.

There is a lot of evidence, however, that in refined Renaissance society the role and importance of women improved. Women such as Beatrice and Isabella d'Este were educated and came to dominate intellectual life. A number of women, such as Antonia Uccello (the daughter of Paolo Uccello, see page 15), became successful artists, and there were several female humanists and poets; the sixteenth-century poet Laura Battiferri was described as having 'a soul of steel and a body of ice'.

A few women achieved success on men's terms. In 1500, Caterina Sforza, who became

ruler of the town of Forlì when her husband died, defended it fiercely against the military leader Cesare Borgia (see page 34) until all was lost. She tried to blow herself up with gunpowder, but when the fuse failed to ignite, bravely coped with capture, rape and imprisonment. Throughout her life she took great care of her looks and in her book *Experiments* wrote of poisons as well as potions to maintain beauty. Renaissance writers considered her to be the complete woman.

In *The Courtier*, one of the men, Giuliano de' Medici, declares that 'all of us know that it is fitting for the courtier to have the greatest reverence for women...a serious woman, strengthened by virtue and insight, acts as a shield against the insolence and beastliness of arrogant men'. A Renaissance gentleman knew how to treat a lady.

The question is, how many gentlemen - and indeed, how many ladies - were there in Renaissance times? Everyday life was often brutal and violent, although the novelist Matteo Bandello (*c.* 1485–1561) probably exaggerated the violence in domestic life when he wrote: 'Nowadays, we see a woman poison her husband [or] send her lover to murder her husband...Every day we hear that a man has murdered his wife because he thought her unfaithful.'

Below: although many rich Renaissance women are well educated, Dorotea Bucca (1400–36) is remarkably successful; she becomes lecturer in medicine at the University of Bologna.

Right: a self-portrait by Sofonisba Anguissola, whose father, unusually, apprentices her to an artist. In 1559 she becomes a portrait painter at the court of the king of Spain.

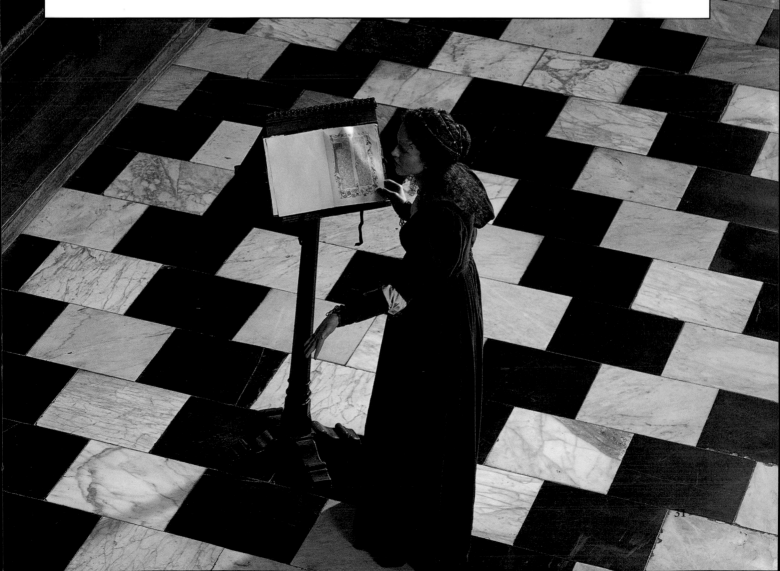

Violence and Intrigue

It is remarkable that the explosion of creativity during the Renaissance took place against a background not of refinement and culture but of war and violence.

For the first half of the fifteenth century, until the Peace of Lodi (1454), the states of Italy were constantly at war. Each state employed mercenaries (hired soldiers) to attack the others. Even that paragon of virtue, Duke Federico of Urbino, made his fortune from selling his services as a soldier to the governments of the other Italian states.

The princes of the tiny Italian states were notoriously vicious. There was no acceptance, as there is today, that rulers had a duty to ensure the well-being of their subjects. Most Italian princes were mainly concerned with staying in power and increasing the power of their families. King Ferrante of Naples governed his kingdom through terror and violence. He embalmed the bodies of those opponents he had put to death, as a gruesome trophy and as a warning to others. Galeazzo Maria Sforza, Duke of Milan (ruled 1466–76), who was obsessed with the beauty of his own hands and voice, humiliated his prisoners by forcing them to eat excrement. He was stabbed to death by three assassins at the end of a church service. In 1494 his brother Lodovico Sforza gained control of the duchy of Milan by poisoning his nephew. In Ferrara, Ercole d'Este poisoned his wife when he thought she was conspiring against him. Sigismondo Malatesta was said to have murdered his first two wives, and to have raped both his daughter and his son. These were the same rulers who were pouring money into humanist studies and exquisite works of art and architecture.

In about 1516 the former Chancellor of

Florence, Niccolò Machiavelli (1469–1527), wrote *The Prince* for Lorenzo the Magnificent's grandson, also called Lorenzo, who was Duke of Urbino from 1516 to 1519. The book advised the young duke on how to survive in such a world. His advice was candid: although it might be beneficial to seem to be a good man, it was better to be feared than loved; successful rulers were ruthless, and the best security was a strong army. Force, fraud and broken promises were acceptable, claimed Machiavelli, as long as they kept the ruler in power, and a wise ruler destroyed the people's freedom before they destroyed him.

Main picture: in this painting by Giovanni Bellini (*c.* 1430–1516) woodcutters ignore an assassination; violence is so common that it is unremarkable.

Right: in an attempt to discourage crime, the brutal punishments for even relatively minor offences such as burglary include torture, burning and hanging - as in this painting by Pisanello (*c.* 1395–1455).

The Papacy

In Renaissance times it was not thought strange that the pope - who was the spiritual leader of the Catholic world - was also the ruler of the Papal States, a belt of land across the centre of Italy. The capital city of this small despotism was Rome, where the popes lived in the Vatican palace.

The popes showed the same interest in Renaissance culture as the other rulers of Italy. Pope Nicholas V (reigned 1447–55) was the first humanist pope. He was an able scholar who employed Alberti to rebuild bridges and the Vergine aqueduct in Rome. His collection of nine thousand books and manuscripts formed the basis of the Vatican library, and he advised both Cosimo de' Medici and Federico of Urbino on how to set up their libraries. He even employed the humanist scholar Lorenzo Valla (see page 9) in the Vatican offices. Pius II (reigned 1458–64) was also a humanist scholar before he became pope, and Sixtus IV (reigned 1471–84) was a typical Renaissance ruler who employed artists such as Ghirlandaio, Botticelli and Mantegna. Sixtus also built the Sistine Chapel (which was named after him) in the Vatican.

Yet Sixtus and his successor Alexander VI (reigned 1492–1503) were arguably the most corrupt rulers in Italy. Sixtus promoted family and friends to important Church positions - he even made one of his servants, an uneducated 20-year-old man, Bishop of Parma in 1463. In 1478 Sixtus supported a plot to assassinate Lorenzo the Magnificent and his brother Giuliano during Mass. When the professional cut-throat, who had begun to admire Lorenzo, refused to do the deed, the conspirators recruited two willing priests.

Alexander was even worse. Machiavelli commented that 'he never did anything else but tell lies…and break promises'. In Rome, Alexander lived in the greatest luxury. His mistress was only 14 when he seduced her from her husband. When he became pope he installed her in rooms next to St Peter's Church in the Vatican, so that he could visit her through a secret door. He scandalized the Romans by having her portrait painted, as the Virgin Mary, on his bedroom wall.

Alexander loaded honours upon his son Cesare Borgia (1476–1507). Cesare was an able commander but he was violent and treacherous. His military campaigns to reduce the nobles of the Papal States to obedience (1499–1503) were so ruthless that they led Machiavelli to use Cesare as the model for his ideal prince. On one occasion, it was claimed, Alexander and his daughter Lucrezia watched Cesare killing criminals by firing arrows at them. They laughed as the men ran around frantically, trying to avoid being hit. It was said that Cesare had murdered his brother and competed with his father to sleep with his sister.

Many historians frankly disbelieve stories such as these (see page 63). Even so, it is clear that Alexander lived in a way which, for a pope, we find shocking today. The Dutch humanist Desiderius Erasmus (c. 1469–1536) called the papacy 'the disease of Christendom'.

The behaviour of the popes tainted the Catholic Church. To some people it seemed as though the entire Church was evil. A priest called Niccolò de' Pelegati was executed in Ferrara in 1495. He had killed five men, taken two wives and was the leader of a notorious band of robbers. Rome was 'a sink of all the vices', according to Lorenzo the Magnificent; in 1490 it had 6,800 official public prostitutes (one-fifth of the population of the city.)

Alexander's death was in keeping with his life. He invited a cardinal to a meal, intending to poison him. However, he drank from the wrong cup and killed himself by mistake.

A cardinal places the papal crown on the head of the pope, who carries a crook symbolizing his position as shepherd of the Catholic Church.

The pope claims to speak with the authority of God when he speaks *ex cathedra* (from his throne).

The Invasions of Italy

For half a century after the Peace of Lodi the Italian states were relatively peaceful. For most of the fifteenth century the other countries of Europe were kept occupied with their own problems; Italy was left free to develop the Renaissance. Unknown to the Italians, however, events were moving towards disaster. In the late fifteenth century there appeared on the world stage two powerful, greedy nations who saw in Italy an opportunity for territorial expansion.

France was becoming a major power. In 1453 the French had finally driven the English out of France, in 1482 they had regained the territories lost to Burgundy and in 1490 they had gained control of Brittany. Charles VIII of France (ruled 1483–98) was young and ambitious, and wanted to win himself a reputation. Meanwhile, Spain had been united through the marriage of Ferdinand of Aragon to Isabella of Castile, and in 1492 the armies of Spain had finally conquered Granada.

In Italy, in 1492, Lorenzo the Magnificent died. It was he, wrote Machiavelli, who had 'put a stop to the internal wars of Italy, and by his wisdom and authority kept peace'. The states of Italy began to quarrel.

In 1493 Lodovico Sforza, the Regent of Milan, found himself without allies and appealed to Charles VIII for help. This gave Charles his excuse to intervene. In 1494 he invaded, claiming his right to the Kingdom of Naples. The Italian mercenaries were no match for the French cannons. In some places the French were welcomed as liberators by citizens sick of tyrannical government. In Florence the towns-people, led by the fiery preacher Girolamo Savonarola (1452–98), rebelled and drove out the Medici family. Charles entered Naples on 22 February 1495 and was crowned king in May. Then he fought his way back to France. Behind him, all the territories he had conquered were gradually lost.

The French invaded again in 1499–1503, 1511–13 and 1515–16. Italy remained a theatre of war until 1559. Cities were sacked and their inhabitants massacred. There were typhus epidemics in 1505 and 1528, and in the 1520s there was an outbreak of the plague. The war also coincided with an outbreak of syphilis (a sexually transmitted disease) which the large armies spread rapidly throughout the country.

These disasters were the beginning of the end of the Renaissance, which was to culminate in the Sack of Rome in 1527 (see page 57). Yet the period from 1495–1527 is usually called the High Renaissance, because it marks the time of the highest achievements of the Renaissance.

It is impossible to know why this paradox occurred. The great sums of money spent on the war temporarily increased the wealth of Italy; Leonardo da Vinci certainly found work designing war machines at this time. Also, as often happens, the war stimulated debate and ideas. The horrors of war caused many Italians to despair and this was mirrored in art and literature - Machiavelli's *Prince*, in particular, reflects the cynicism of the time.

Right: an Italian mercenary.
Below: at the battle of Pavia (1525) the forces of the Holy Roman Emperor, Charles V, defeat the French armies and capture the French king, Francis I.

Leonardo da Vinci

Pope Leo X once exclaimed about Leonardo da Vinci, 'Alas, this man will never get anything done'. All that remains from the 67 years of Leonardo's life are a dozen paintings, a few illustrated fables and his notebooks. Yet as a young man Leonardo had written confidently: 'I wish to work miracles.'

Leonardo began his career as an apprentice to Andrea del Verrocchio (see page 18) who once asked his pupil to add an angel to a painting he had been working on, called *The Baptism of Christ*. According to legend, after comparing Leonardo's angel to his own work, Verrocchio decided to concentrate on sculpture.

In about 1482 Leonardo went to work for Lodovico Sforza in Milan. He was kept busy designing costumes and scenery for the court entertainments. He also designed a central heating system, new military machines (his ideas included a tank, a huge crossbow, life jackets and a parachute), town plans and irrigation schemes. The nature of much of the work he was commissioned to do meant that little survived. It has been proved that many of his inventions, such as the tank, would not have worked, and his towns were never built.

In 1499, after a change of alliances, the French attacked Lodovico and drove him out of Milan. Leonardo went to Florence where, in 1503, he suffered three spectacular failures. Commissioned to paint a huge fresco of *The Battle of Anghiari*, he decided to try a new paint mixture and a kind of plaster described by the Roman writer Pliny. The result was disastrous - the paint never dried and the colours ran into each other. A flying machine he had designed crashed, breaking the leg of his pupil Zoroastro, who had been brave enough to test it. A scheme to divert the River Arno had to be abandoned when, after two thousand workmen had started work, Leonardo discovered a mistake in his calculations.

Main picture: unusually for Renaissance times, Leonardo is a vegetarian and cannot bear to see animals in pain. He believes horses to be almost supernatural and does many detailed drawings of them.

In 1493 Leonardo completes a full-size clay model for an equestrian statue of Lodovico's father, Francesco Sforza, but the statue is never made because Lodovico takes the bronze to make cannons to fight the invading French armies. French gunners ruin the model by using it for target practice. Only Leonardo's preliminary drawings (left) survive from the project.

Art and Science

Although many of Leonardo da Vinci's projects were unsuccessful (see page 38), he was renowned in his own time and many artists were influenced by him. His sketches of churches formed the basis of Bramante's design for the new St Peter's Church in Rome (see page 43). Many art historians date the period they call the High Renaissance from around 1495, when Leonardo began to paint *The Last Supper*, and some historians assert that Leonardo da Vinci changed the course, not only of art, but of the Renaissance.

The Science of Art

Leonardo was responsible for three important developments in painting.

Firstly, his treatment of light was revolutionary. His knowledge of light allowed him to develop the techniques of *chiaroscuro* (light and shade) and *sfumato* (softening of the edges). This gave his paintings the sense of gentleness and mystery that fascinates everybody who sees, for instance, the *Mona Lisa*.

Secondly, his understanding of light and human movement enabled him to depict, as he said, 'the intention of men's souls'. His fresco of *The Last Supper* successfully portrays his subjects' emotions, from the guilt of Judas

Iscariot to the resignation of Jesus Christ, who accepts his destiny with a shrug.

Thirdly, Leonardo did detailed research for his paintings. He was not content to depict the outside of things; he wanted to see inside them to understand why they worked as they did. He dissected more than ten corpses in order to understand the anatomy of the human body. He filled his notebooks with sketches and preliminary drawings. The knowledge he gained allowed him to create masterpieces.

The Art of Science

Leonardo's research for his paintings had led him to conduct what were in fact scientific investigations. 'Art truly is a science,' he explained. His notebooks are filled with

left-handed mirror writing describing his observations and discoveries. He spent weeks experimenting with flies, trimming their wings or putting honey on them to study how this changed the sound of the buzzing. He made a particular study of the flight of birds. Later, he became obsessed with mathematics. In 1509 he illustrated a book by the mathematician Luca Pacioli (1445–1517) called *The Divine Proportion*. Pacioli had calculated that the perfect ratio was 1:1·6 and that a rectangle of these proportions (the shape of a piece of foolscap paper) was the shape most pleasing to the eye. This concept, which Leonardo renamed the golden section, is still studied by artists and mathematicians.

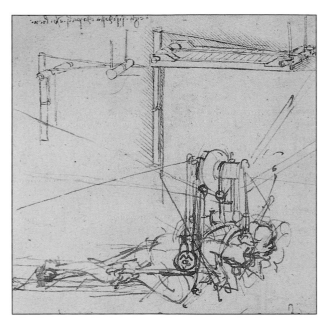

Leonardo rejected the medieval view of science which held that nature was controlled by spiritual powers, and that, for instance, it was the soul of a bird which allowed it to fly. 'A bird is an instrument working according to mathematical law,' he wrote. Leonardo insisted that observation and experiments were the only way to find out the truth about nature. In this, he can be said to be the founder of modern science. It was his obsession with new ideas that led to the failure of some of his projects.

This obsession also marks a major change in the direction of the Renaissance. Before Leonardo, artists and scholars had been content to imitate the Greeks and Romans; in the words of one modern historian, they had tried to recover the past. After Leonardo da Vinci, during the High Renaissance, artists and scholars tried to discover new things.

Leonardo always felt he had failed. In his old age he covered his notebooks with the comment 'Tell me if anything at all was achieved'. Yet in certain ways Leonardo da Vinci changed the world.

Above left: Leonardo's angel in *The Virgin of the Rocks* (*c.* 1506) illustrates his mastery of the techniques of *chiaroscuro* and *sfumato*.

Main picture: Leonardo's fresco of *The Last Supper*; Judas sits fourth from the left. Unfortunately, Leonardo experiments with a mixture of oil and tempera, which almost immediately begins to flake off the plaster.

Left: the flying machine sketched in Leonardo's notebook is reminiscent of a modern hang-glider.

The Roman Renaissance

According to a modern historian, during the fifteenth century the city of Rome became 'the centre of Western civilization'. The popes lived in Rome, which made it the administrative centre of the Catholic Church. From all over western Europe, Church taxes flowed into the city. Rome became a diplomatic centre and a flourishing banking centre. Finally, during the reign of Pope Julius II (1503–13), Rome replaced Florence as the centre of the High Renaissance.

The popes were great patrons of the arts. Julius employed the architect Bramante to redesign St Peter's Church. He persuaded Michelangelo to paint the Sistine Chapel (see page 46) and commissioned Raphael to decorate his rooms in the Vatican (see page 48). He also entertained many humanist scholars.

Julius's successor, Leo X (reigned 1513–21), was the son of Lorenzo the Magnificent. Leo's reign as pope is often called the golden age of the Renaissance. On becoming pope, it was alleged, Leo told a friend: 'Let us enjoy the papacy.' He supported a vast number of poets, artists and scholars, and spent eight thousand ducats a month on presents for his favourites (and on gambling). He set up a school of Greek in Rome, and expanded the university until it had more than a hundred teachers.

Leo loved music. When he became pope many of the singers in Mantua left for Rome to seek his patronage. He employed 15 composers, including the lute-player Gian Maria Giuldeo, who was paid 23 ducats a month and raised to the rank of count.

A major rebuilding programme was started in Rome during the time of Leo X. The Vatican was extended and decorated. Leo also knocked down a great deal of the old medieval housing to create large squares and give a better view of the surviving Roman architecture. He spent so much that he emptied the papal treasury, and when he died owing 622,000 ducats he almost ruined the bankers of Rome.

Meanwhile, the cardinals of the Church and Roman bankers such as the papal treasurer Agostino Chigi (1465–1520) poured money into art and architecture. Thousands of workers came to Rome from Milan to build cardinals' palaces, merchants' mansions and new churches. Whereas in 1503 there had been only eight painters living in the city of Rome, in 1528 the Fraternity of St Luke (the guild of painters in the city) had 124 members.

In Rome, bankers, nobles and churchmen live extravagantly. One rich Roman uses silver plates, ostentatiously throwing them into the River Tiber after each course. Unknown to his guests he has placed a net on the river bed, so he can recover the plates.

Here, during a lavish meal, the pope discusses a commission with an artist. The pope's food taster stands behind him.

Michelangelo

Even in his lifetime 'the divine Michelangelo' - sculptor, painter, architect and poet - was held to be a genius. His character fulfils our stereotype of a genius: brilliant yet difficult,

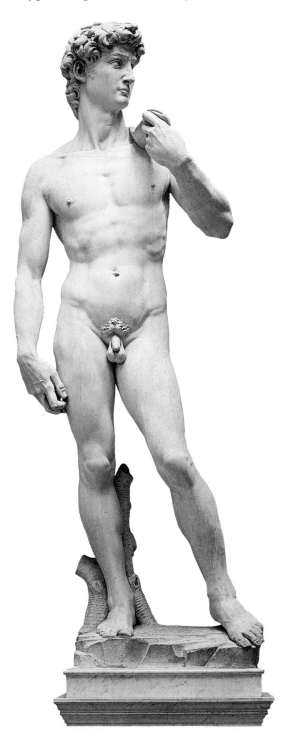

outspoken and unstable. He was often sweaty and dishevelled, and slept in his boots. He criticized other artists. Once he was so rude that an apprentice punched him and broke his nose. On another occasion Leonardo da Vinci asked Michelangelo to explain a passage of poetry to some admirers. 'Explain it yourself - you who made a model of a bronze horse and could not even cast it,' snapped Michelangelo. He cared little for the wishes of his patrons, and often put a clause in his contracts which gave him the right to do the work 'as it pleases the said Michelangelo'. Once, when the pope would not see him, Michelangelo left Rome for seven months. According to a story told by Michelangelo, when asked why he had left, he told the pope: 'Not from ill will, but from scorn.'

Michelangelo learned his skills while apprenticed to the painter Ghirlandaio in Florence. He sketched classical statues in the Medici gardens, and imitated them so success-fully that his sculpture of a sleeping Cupid was sold by a dealer as a genuine antique.

Like Leonardo da Vinci, Michelangelo changed the way artists painted. Although he understood the rules of perspective and foreshortening (see page 15), he demanded the right to ignore them when he wanted to create a particular effect. 'All the reasonings of geometry and arithmetic and all the proofs of perspective are of no use to a man without the eye,' he remarked. After he had carved the tomb of Giuliano de' Medici (1534), it was observed that the figure on the tomb did not look like the dead man. 'A thousand years from now, nobody will want to know what he really looked like,' retorted Michelangelo. Out of this attitude came a new style of painting which art historians call Mannerism; mannerists broke the rules in order to achieve a desired effect.

Michelangelo also helped to change the whole direction of the Renaissance, which after 1520 lost its confident and joyful attitude to humanity, sex and nature (see page 22). Michelangelo's works were awe-inspiring, but they were also solemn and religious. In later life his sculptures conveyed a sense of human weakness, sin, sadness and death.

Michelangelo died at the age of 89. He was an example of the Renaissance 'universal man', whose talents covered a vast range of subjects. He wrote poetry in a neat Renaissance italic script. His skills as an architect were so respected that in 1546 he was put in charge of the rebuilding of St Peter's Church in Rome.

Right: Michelangelo believes that the figure already exists within the block, and that his job is simply to free it by chipping away the stone. He does this from the front, carving the figure out of the stone as if he is lifting it from a tank of water. His unfinished statue of a slave looks as though it is struggling to free itself from the stone which imprisons it.

Left: the statue of David by Michelangelo is more than 4.25 metres (14 feet) tall.

Above left: Michelangelo does much to popularize the cult of the Virgin Mary in Italy. His *Pietà*, sculpted in 1498–99, shows Mary as a young woman, 'to prove to the world the...perpetual purity of the Virgin'.

Background picture: Michelangelo uses marble from the quarries at Carrara, 80 miles (130 kilometres) from Florence.

The Sistine Chapel

In 1508 Pope Julius II asked Michelangelo to paint the ceiling of the Sistine Chapel in the Vatican. Michelangelo accepted the job against his wishes; he claimed that he was a sculptor, not a painter.

The huge fresco (see pages 1–5) took Michelangelo four years to complete. Too much of a perfectionist to employ assistants, he worked mostly alone, leaning over backwards on scaffolding which reached right up to the ceiling. In a poem written in 1510, he described how uncomfortable the work was:

My belly is shoved up under my chin…
My beard faces skywards and the back of my neck
*   is wedged into my spine…*
My face is richly carpeted with a thick layer of
*   paint from my brush…*
I don't want to be here and I'm no painter.

The relationship between the temperamental artist and the fierce pope was stormy. Julius frequently climbed up to inspect the work and once, when Michelangelo told him he would finish 'when I can', Julius threatened to throw Michelangelo from the scaffolding.

The Sistine Chapel ceiling comprises 340 figures and 520 square metres (5,600 square feet) of plaster.

The biblical scenes show the story of creation in reverse order. Starting with Noah lying drunk and disgraced, they continue with the Flood, Noah's sacrifice, Adam and Eve being cast out of the Garden of Eden, and the creation of Eve, Adam (see main picture), the sky and water, the sun and moon, and light. In this way, visitors who walk through the chapel literally leave behind them the sins of this world and make their way towards God.

Right: Michelangelo's sketch shows how he had to stand to paint the frescoes.

Raphael

Compared with the feckless Leonardo and the irascible Michelangelo, Raphael was the model of a Renaissance courtier. The son of an artist at the court of Urbino, he wrote poetry and was a friend of Castiglione. Many people thought he would eventually be made a cardinal. Vasari called him 'a mortal god'.

In 1508 Raphael went to Rome, where Julius II commissioned him to paint a number of rooms in the Vatican, notably the Stanza della Segnatura. The pope's aim, one modern historian has written, was to show 'the authority, teaching and leadership of the papacy and the Catholic Church'. For instance, *The Mass at Bolsena*, a painting of a doubting priest who was finally convinced that the bread and wine had become the true body and blood of Christ, was painted to discourage those

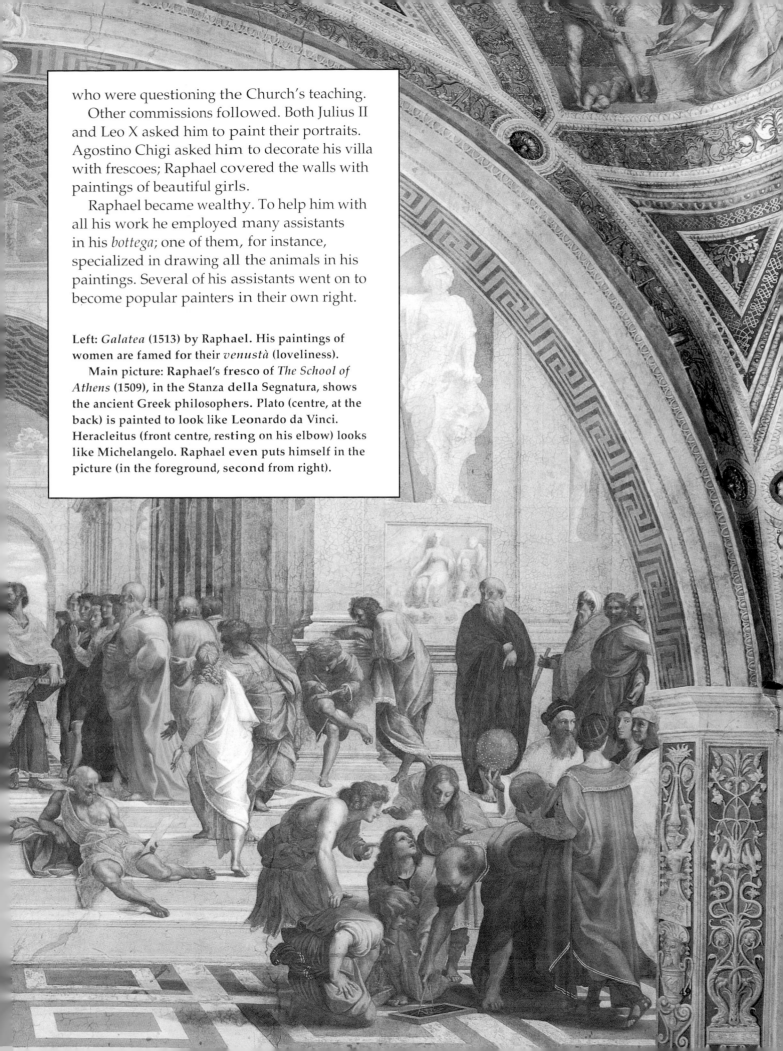

who were questioning the Church's teaching.

Other commissions followed. Both Julius II and Leo X asked him to paint their portraits. Agostino Chigi asked him to decorate his villa with frescoes; Raphael covered the walls with paintings of beautiful girls.

Raphael became wealthy. To help him with all his work he employed many assistants in his *bottega*; one of them, for instance, specialized in drawing all the animals in his paintings. Several of his assistants went on to become popular painters in their own right.

Left: *Galatea* (1513) by Raphael. His paintings of women are famed for their *venustà* (loveliness).

Main picture: Raphael's fresco of *The School of Athens* (1509), in the Stanza della Segnatura, shows the ancient Greek philosophers. Plato (centre, at the back) is painted to look like Leonardo da Vinci. Heracleitus (front centre, resting on his elbow) looks like Michelangelo. Raphael even puts himself in the picture (in the foreground, second from right).

Music

During the Renaissance, music was an essential part of church ceremonies and court life. It was also a common form of entertainment for ordinary people.

Renaissance writers believed that composers such as Guillaume Dufay (1400–74) and Josquin Desprez (*c.* 1440–1521) had improved music as much as artists such as Donatello and Michelangelo had changed painting and sculpture. In the 1470s, Johannes de Tinctoris (*c.* 1435–1511), a Netherlander living in Italy, claimed that 'there does not exist a single piece of music…worth hearing which was not composed within the last forty years'.

The musicians of the Renaissance could not copy Greek or Roman music because it had never been written down. They could, however, read the theories of the Greek philosopher Pythagoras, who said that harmony ought to be based on mathematical intervals, especially thirds and fifths (the notes which are two and four tones above the bass note). Renaissance composers used these ideas to develop the principles of counterpoint (combining voices in harmony). For the dedication of the dome of Florence Cathedral (see page 17) Dufay wrote *Nuper rosarum flores*, a piece of music with harmonies based on the ratios used by Brunelleschi in his design of the dome.

Later in the Renaissance musicians began to compose all the parts at the same time to emphasize the way the voices merged together in harmony. Instruments such as the harpsichord and the lute (on which chords could be played) became popular. There was also a new respect

for the meaning of the words and their mood. Late Renaissance composers often based their music around a simple tune, which was repeated in turn by the different parts. Renaissance music, therefore, achieved a beautiful, complex intertwining of tunes and harmonies.

At first, Renaissance music was dominated by Netherlanders (Josquin was the most famous). It was only towards the end of the sixteenth century that Italian composers such as Pierluigi da Palestrina (*c.* 1525–94) began to make their mark. Even today, music students study Palestrina counterpoint.

Music writing became standardized and in 1501, in Venice, Ottaviano Petrucci printed the first music to show staves, notes and words together. It became socially necessary for courtiers to be able to sing or play music. Isabella d'Este (see page 27) was an accomplished lute player, and it was at her court in Mantua that the *frottola* (a song in four parts) was developed. Composers wrote music for court dances and set the poems of Petrarch and the Roman poet Virgil to music. The desire of musicians to put poetry to music led also to the development of the madrigal, a more complex composition for voices and, sometimes, instruments. Finally, during the sixteenth century, a group of Florentine musicians - the *Camerata fiorentina* - met to try to develop a form of music similar to that used in the classical world. This movement led, late in the century, to the development of opera.

A group of late-Renaissance musicians. The two singers facing one another are accompanied by (left to right) bass viol, lute, another bass viol, recorder, cornetto and chitarrone (archlute).

Theatre

In medieval Europe, township guilds had performed miracle and mystery plays which had religious themes. The theatre as we know it today developed in Renaissance Italy.

The first step was the discovery by humanist scholars of the Greek tragedies and comedies, which they tried to imitate. The architect Alberti wrote a comedy in Latin which was mistaken for a classical play. Authors started to use secular themes; for instance, they produced spectacles (for celebrations such as weddings) and court entertainments which involved enactments of the legends of King Arthur or famous historical events. When, as a result, the Church refused to let the actors perform on the church steps, they used carts or balconies instead. In 1580 the Italian architect Andrea Palladio (1508–80, see page 61) designed the first permanent theatre, in Vicenza.

In the sixteenth century the first plays were written in the Italian language. *Sofonisba*, by the Italian playwright Giangiorgio Trissino (1478–1550) was the first to be successful. Niccolò Machiavelli wrote two bawdy plays in Italian - *Clizia* (inspired by the Roman writer Plautus) and *La Mandragola* (the Mandrake Root), which was said by one writer of the

time to 'carry away the prize for originality'.

As the theatre developed, so did the art of acting, especially after about 1550, when women were first allowed to perform on stage. A Renaissance actor needed a clear, loud voice, and the ability to show emotion (usually this meant extreme over-acting). They improvised their speeches and added jokes to the script to keep the audience entertained. Venice was the centre of this development. Particularly famous were Angelo Beolco (who wrote in the Paduan dialect and was nicknamed 'the bumpkin') and the actress Vincenza Armani, a sixteenth-century beauty who wrote perfect Latin and composed music to accompany her own poems.

Theatre becomes so popular that 'workers go without food to have the money to go to the play'. They especially enjoy the *commedia dell'arte*, a form of comic theatre in which the first clowns appear. One character, Pulcinella, becomes the Punch of later Punch and Judy shows, while Harlequin (right) is a slow-witted servant who is an excellent acrobat. If the actor playing Harlequin runs out of things to say, he hits other actors with his stick!

Main picture: theatre is also influenced by carnivals such as this festival in Siena.

Changes in Religion

It would be wrong to present the Renaissance as an unchristian age. Throughout Europe, especially in Italy, millions of ordinary men and women tried to live according to their Christian beliefs.

Nevertheless, the Renaissance was a difficult time for the Christian religion. Humanists such as Valla discovered that the Vulgate Bible - used by the Catholic Church since the fourth century - contained mistranslations and errors (see page 9). Scholars who read Greek texts learned about the Greek gods. During one church service at which Pope Leo X was present, the speaker absent-mindedly prayed to the Greek immortals (the Greek gods)! Other Renaissance humanists believed that their lives were dominated by the stars (astrology), read occult writings and practised magic, alchemy or witchcraft.

At the same time, there was increasing dissatisfaction with the Catholic Church. Guicciardini, who had been secretary to Leo X, called the papal court 'a disgrace, an example of all the shames and scandals of the world. It would be impossible to say too many bad things about it'.

Eventually there was disaster. It hinged upon money. Pope Leo needed millions of ducats for his luxurious lifestyle and architectural projects (notably the rebuilding of St Peter's in Rome). His methods of raising money became increasingly disreputable. In 1517 he arrested a number of cardinals who he claimed were plotting to assassinate him. He had one of them strangled, then set the rest free after they had paid fines of up to 150,000 ducats. Soon after, Leo created 31 new cardinals, after each of them had paid him more than 300,000 ducats.

There was an outcry. Machiavelli thought that 'the Church's ruin and punishment are at

hand'. The criticism was strongest in Germany where, as Leo had been warned in 1516, thousands were waiting for a chance to speak out against the pope.

The chance came in 1517 when Leo's agent Johann Tetzel arrived in the German town of Wittenberg in Saxony. He was selling papal indulgences (pardons which promised the buyer forgiveness from any sin) to raise money for the Archbishop of Mainz, who had just bought his archbishopric from Leo X. Half the sum raised by Tetzel was to go towards the rebuilding of St Peter's Church in Rome. 'The holy Father had the power to forgive sin and, if he forgave it, God must do so also,' Tetzel preached.

This approach outraged an Augustinian monk called Martin Luther (1483–1546). On 31 October 1517 Luther nailed his Ninety-five Theses (a series of documents criticizing Tetzel) to the door of the Castle Church in Wittenberg. Luther argued that it was not good deeds that saved the believer from hell (as Tetzel claimed) but faith in Jesus Christ. In 1520, Leo issued a papal bull (law) declaring Luther a heretic. Nothing could be done, however, because the Duke of Saxony, seeing an opportunity to free himself from the authority of the pope, protected Luther.

Other German states - Hesse, Brunswick and Brandenburg - broke with Rome, as did Denmark and Sweden. Henry VIII of England also defied the pope when he was refused permission to divorce his wife. Protestantism had been born.

A seventeenth-century painting of an alchemist's laboratory. Alchemists study the works of the so-called Hermes Trismegistus (written in the third century AD), which teach that the universe is held together by occult forces. They try to control these forces by means of spells, charms and symbolic pictures. In this way they hope to find the philosopher's stone which will help them control nature and give them the secret of everlasting life and health.

The Sack of Rome

Modern historians have blamed the popes for the misfortunes of the Catholic Church during the Renaissance. The popes threw away their spiritual authority by living scandalous and extravagant lives, and tried to wield temporal (worldy) power like any other ruler of the time. In the early sixteenth century the pope ruled one of the most powerful states in Italy. However, he was weak compared to the two rulers who wanted to dominate Italy - Francis I, the King of France, and Charles V who was not only the Duke of Burgundy and the Netherlands but also the Holy Roman Emperor and the King of Spain.

Despite this, Pope Clement VII (reigned 1523–34) schemed to compete with these powers in world politics. When Francis invaded Italy in 1524, Clement supported him against Charles. The result was three years of war, which ruined much of Italy.

In the spring of 1527, Charles assembled in Milan a large force of German mercenaries and some Spanish troops, under the command of Charles de Bourbon. That year, however, Francis could not afford to send an army, so Clement was left without an ally.

Charles's army marched south to Rome. On 6 May 1527 the soldiers broke through the walls and swarmed into the city. Bourbon was killed in the first assault, so his men - many of whom were Lutherans - ransacked the city. For eight days they killed, raped and looted without mercy, and destroyed many of the frescoes and statues. Monks and nuns were treated with particular brutality. Cardinals were dragged round the houses of their friends, begging loans to pay the ransoms demanded for their lives; then they were taken round again. Women threw themselves from windows to avoid being raped and fathers stabbed their daughters to death to save them from the mob.

While Clement took refuge in the castle of Sant'Angelo, Lutherans paraded through the streets of Rome with their leader dressed as the pope sitting on a donkey. When a priest refused their demands to give the donkey Communion, they tortured him to death. Looters opened the tomb of St Peter, looking for gold, and one of the German soldiers attached to his own spear the lance-head said to have pierced the side of Christ. The Vatican was used as a stable, and papal bulls and manuscripts were used as bedding for the horses.

Charles's army occupied Rome for nine months. It was said that during that time two thousand bodies were thrown into the River Tiber, ten thousand were buried, and money and treasures worth four million ducats were looted. The soldiers, said a writer of the time, had made Rome 'a stinking slaughterhouse'; the smell of rotting corpses lingered for months afterwards.

Although the city recovered quite quickly and soon regained its position as the centre of the Catholic Church, the Sack of Rome was a disaster for the papacy. It destroyed once and for all the claim made since the Middle Ages that the rulers of the world owed allegiance to the pope. Contemporaries called it 'a judgement from God', and when Clement died, the people of Rome lit bonfires to celebrate, dragging his body into the streets and mutilating it.

The Sack of Rome also undermined the carefree confidence which characterized Renaissance art. Many historians believe the Sack of Rome marked the end of the Renaissance.

Lutheran soldiers, wearing cardinals' robes over their armour, loot and burn churches and murder the priests.

The Renaissance Survives

After the Sack of Rome many scholars and artists fled to Venice, which became a centre of Renaissance scholarship and the arts in the later sixteenth century.

Venice was a great trading city. Its merchants made their fortunes by selling the luxury goods of the East (silks and spices) to the rich nobles of the West. Every year, six fleets of trading ships were sent out - in all, 330 ships with thirty-six thousand crewmen. They went to the Black Sea, Greece, Syria, Egypt and north Africa, as well as to England and Flanders. The Venetian Arsenal (dockyard) was the largest industrial concern in western Europe, employing thousands of workmen. The Arsenal used assembly-line techniques and during one period of war was able to build a new ship every day for a hundred days. Every vessel had standardized fittings (oars, masts and sails, for instance) and replacement parts were kept in ports all over the known world.

According to one modern historian, the government of Venice was 'the admiration and the envy of Europe'. It consisted of an elected doge (duke), an elected Great Council, a Senate of 120 members which made laws and directed foreign affairs, and a very powerful Council of Ten which administered the every-day affairs of state. The second agenda item at every meeting of the Council of Ten was the 'denunciations', the trial of those suspected of treachery. Any citizen could denounce his or her neighbours by writing their names on a piece of paper and putting it through a hole shaped like a lion's mouth in the wall of the doge's palace. The accused were arrested and tried by the Council of Ten. They were held to be guilty until they proved themselves to be innocent. Those who failed to do so were hanged, beheaded, buried alive or strangled,

and their bodies dumped quietly in a part of the lagoon reserved for the purpose.

Venice became a place of culture, scandal and extravagance. The doge and the rich merchants of Venice could afford to patronize the arts. Painters such as Titian (*c.* 1490–1576) painted their portraits. The architect Palladio built villas for them all over the *Terraferma* (the area of mainland Italy ruled by Venice). The writer Pietro Aretino (1492–1556) lived in Venice after 1527, and amused and shocked wealthy Venetians with his books and plays, some of which were pornographic. Also at this time, the mainland town of Padua (in Venetian territory) had the only university medical school in Europe that insisted its students must visit the sick as part of their training.

Venice became especially famous for its music. Large numbers of professional singers and players were brought from all over Europe to perform at St Mark's Cathedral. Musicians strove to achieve the most beautiful sounds and harmonies possible. This affected Palladio's church designs, which were the first to take into account the acoustics of a building (the way a building affects sound).

Although they were Catholics, the people of Venice had never fully accepted the authority of the papacy. Many Venetians had adopted the 'modern devotion' of Erasmus, who had come to Venice in 1508 to work with Aldus Manutius. Venetian bishops led a movement to reform the Catholic Church and in 1536 Pope Paul III asked a Venetian, Gasparo Contarini, to head a commission to look into the Church's problems. The commission marked the beginning of the process of reform called the Counter-Reformation, which was to save the Roman Catholic Church from collapse.

During the Renaissance, Venetian artists begin to use bright oil paints and to pay great attention to detail, as in this painting by Leandro Bassano of trade and traffic along the waterways of Venice.

Results of the Renaissance

During the sixteenth century the Italian Renaissance spread to the rest of Europe.

France and Spain attracted the cream of Italian talent; for instance, Leonardo da Vinci went to France to work for Francis I, and Charles V was painted by Titian. The less-well-known artists went to other countries. After breaking Michelangelo's nose (see page 44), the sculptor Pietro Torrigiano fled to England to work in Westminster Abbey. The humanist Filippo Callimaco went to Poland where he helped to found a Polish humanist movement. The architect Aristotele Fioravanti designed St Michael's Cathedral in the Kremlin for Tsar Ivan III of Russia.

At the same time, Europe came to Italy. The German artist Albrecht Dürer spent two years in Venice, from 1505 to 1507; he became fascinated with perspective and the shape of the human body, and painted in an Italian style for most of the rest of his life. Martin Luther (see page 55) visited Rome in 1510 - and was horrified. Both the Flemish doctor Andreas Vesalius and the English doctor William Harvey (who discovered how blood circulates round the body) went to Padua University.

In some respects, however, the Renaissance

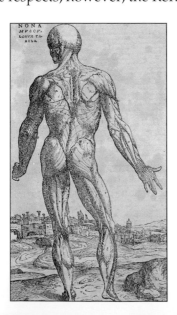

was a disaster. Lorenzo de' Medici and Leo X not only bankrupted themselves, they ruined the states over which they had charge. In religious matters, the Renaissance coincided with a permanent split in western Christianity - between Catholic and Protestant - which was to lead to centuries of wars, persecution, massacres and burnings. In politics, the Renaissance saw the beginnings of aggressive nationalism, of all-powerful rulers, and of 'Machiavellian' politics. These forces still threaten to destroy the world today.

In other ways the developments of the Renaissance benefited humanity.

Renaissance scholars revived the study of archaeology and history. They gave us italic script, foolscap paper, pocket-sized books and many of our ideas about music. They rejected the authority of the Church in matters of learning, and trusted instead the results of their own observations and experiments. This obsession with gaining knowledge formed the basis for the Scientific Revolution of the seventeenth century and the 'Enlightenment' of the eighteenth century. In this way, the Renaissance saw the beginnings of modern mathematics, science and medicine.

The desire to find things out also partly explains the importance of Italians in the European Reconnaissance - the Renaissance exploration of the world. Cristoforo Colombo (1451–1506) was born in Genoa. He was a typical Renaissance man: arrogant, confident and greedy. His studies of geography and history led him to reject the teaching of the Church that the Atlantic Ocean was too wide to be crossed, and in 1492 he set sail from Spain to prove that he was right. His voyage is arguably one of the most important events in the history of the world. But he was not the only Italian involved in exploration. The Florentine explorer Amerigo Vespucci (1454–1512) was the first person to realize that the New World is a continent, and it is after him that America is named. When King Ferdinand of Spain decided in 1508 that only pilots who had passed a navigation examination could take a ship across the Atlantic, he put Vespucci in charge of the examination. In 1497 another Italian, the navigator Giovanni Caboto (known as John Cabot, 1450–98), sailed a British ship to North America. Half a century later his son Sebastian (1476–1557) pioneered a sea route from Britain to Russia.

For three centuries Italian culture dominated people's thinking. Country villas were built in the classical 'Palladian' manner. Grammar schools taught Greek and Latin. People felt that to appear educated they had to appreciate the arts, to read literature and poetry, and to attend the opera and theatre. A tour of Italy was an important part of a gentleman's education, and as late as the nineteenth century, artists such as the British painter J.M.W. Turner (1775–1851) believed that it was essential to spend time in Italy studying the art of the Renaissance.

During the Renaissance, also, polite manners were developed, mainly through the influence of Castiglione's book *The Courtier*. Published in 1528, it was translated into French in 1537, Spanish in 1540 and English in 1561. In 1566 a Polish version appeared, although the translator had edited it so that it was set in Cracow instead of Urbino, and it did not have any women in it. He also omitted the sections on art and sculpture, on the grounds that 'we don't know about them here'!

Nineteenth-century historians believed that the world in which they lived had been influenced and shaped by the developments of the Renaissance. Writing in 1875, J.A. Symonds commented that 'Castiglione's courtier is…a modern gentleman, such as all men of education at the present day would wish to be'.

Left: Vesalius's revolutionary book on anatomy, *The Fabric of the Human Body* (1543), is based on dissections done in Italy. It is illustrated by Jan Steven van Calcar, a German artist living in Italy, and printed in Venice.

Below: the Polish astronomer Nicolaus Copernicus (1473–1543) studies Greek, mathematics and astronomy in the universities of Padua and Bologna; while in Italy he develops the theory that the earth orbits the sun.

How Do We Know?

A great many things have survived from Renaissance times. Historians can study the paintings of artists such as Botticelli (see page 9) or Mantegna (pages 22–3). They can marvel at the beauty of a Donatello statue (page 18) or Michelangelo's awe-inspiring frescoes on the Sistine Chapel ceiling (pages 1–5). Only a few of Leonardo da Vinci's paintings remain, but historians can study his notebooks (page 40). Brunelleschi's dome still dominates the Florence skyline (page 17), and the architecture of Palladio survives, not only in the villas and palaces he built, but in the hundreds of Palladian mansions which were built in imitation throughout western Europe.

Sometimes, also, experts have attempted to re-create Renaissance instruments and artefacts. It is important to remember, however, that the detail of the re-creation depends upon the standpoint of the historian. For example, just before the photograph of the printing press was taken for this book (see page 25), the wood of the press was stained black so that it could be used in a film about Frankenstein.

Perhaps most remarkably of all, while I was writing this book I was able to play modern recordings of music composed by Palestrina (see page 51) and know that I was hearing the same music that cardinals and nobles had listened to more than four centuries ago.

have to remember, however, that the writers might not have been telling the whole truth.

Printing was invented during the Renaissance (see page 24). Large numbers of books were published and eagerly read. One of Luther's books sold four thousand copies in one month in 1520. Inevitably some have survived - especially as it was during the Renaissance that many libraries were set up (see, for example, page 34).

The Renaissance produced some great works of literature, including the letters of Petrarch (see page 8), the philosophy of Erasmus (page 59), the plays of Trissino (page 52), the poetry

Literacy and Literature

There was a general increase in literacy (the ability to read) during Renaissance times, and a far greater number of written sources is available to the historian than for the Middle Ages. Historians can study a vast number of manuscript sources ranging from the business accounts of Florentine merchants to the letter in which Michelangelo boasts about how he put the pope in his place (see page 44). They

of Politian (page 9) and the famous romantic epic *Orlando Furioso* by Ariosto (page 26). Historians can read Machiavelli's plays (page 52), and his bitter book on politics, *The Prince* (page 33), although they have to realize that it was written during a period of despair and failure and is completely uncharacteristic of Machiavelli's beliefs or actions. In the same way, an historian who wants to find out about manners and personal conduct during the Renaissance might read *The Courtier*, but has to realize that Castiglione was writing an idealized account of the discussions at Urbino, 21 years after the event, and that he intended the book to be a manual on 'how to behave'.

The First Historians

The historian of the Renaissance is also lucky enough to have histories written at the time. Biondo and Bracciolini (see page 8) have been described as 'the real founders of modern archaeology', and Renaissance writers revived the writing of history. Alberti (page 15), Cennini (page 20) and Vasari (page 17) have left us histories of Renaissance art and architecture. Bruni (page 10) and Guicciardini (page 26) were not only careful historians, but also held high posts in the government, which allowed them to know what was really going on. Historians have to be aware, however, that Renaissance writers did not try to give the objective truth, but wrote so that their readers might learn the 'lessons of history'.

For this reason, many historians doubt some of the more extreme stories that have come down to us about the rulers of Italy (see pages 32-4). Similarly, the tales of horror from the Sack of Rome may have been exaggerated by writers trying to draw a moral about the corruption of the papacy; no historian, for instance, has ever been able to find the name of a woman who killed herself rather than be raped, or of a father who killed his daughter to save her from the mob (see page 57).

Authority and Freedom of Thought

This book began by noting how differently people thought in medieval times, when the laws of the government and the ideas of the Catholic Church were thought to have the authority of God. The Renaissance overthrew this idea. It accepted that truth is reached through reading and research, and then making up your own mind. Of all the results of the Renaissance, this is perhaps the most important.

Was the Renaissance the beginning of the Modern Age? You should now be able to decide for yourself, but you must bear in mind that the very idea of coming to your own conclusions after you have read about something dates from the Renaissance.

Above left: paintings provide information about life in Renaissance times; for instance, this detail from *The Mass at Bolsena* by Raphael (see page 48) shows the uniform of the Swiss Guard who protected the pope.

Below: an astronomical chart (*c.* 1543) based on Copernicus's theories (see page 61). Renaissance ideas have survived through books published at the time.

Below left: in this diagram the sixteenth-century French humanist Charles de Bouelles (*c.* 1479–1553) suggests that there are four levels of humanity. A lazy person merely exists (in Latin *est*) like a stone. A greedy person might be said to live (*vivit*) like a plant, and a vain person to feel (*sentit*) like an animal. Only the scholar who thinks (*intelligit*) is truly human.

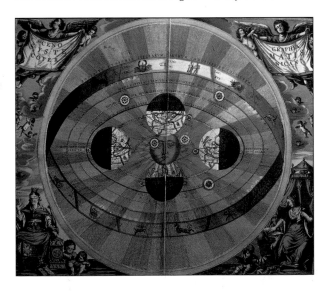

Index

| 1400 | 1410 | 1420 | 1430 | 1440 | 1450 | 1460 | 1470 | 1480 | 1490 | 1500 | 1510 | 1520 | 1530 | 1540 | 1550 | 1560 | 1570 | 1580 | 1590 |

1400-1436 Dorotea Bucca

1450-1498 Giovanni Caboto, explorer

● 1401 Ghiberti wins the competition for the Baptistry doors

● 1402 Death of Gian Galeazzo Visconti

1476-1557 Sebastian Cabot, explorer

● 1478 Sixtus IV's plot to assassinate Lorenzo the Magnificent

● 1454 The Peace of Lodi

● 1493 Lodovico Sforza asks Charles VIII to intervene in Italy

● 12 May 1495 Charles VIII is crowned King of Naples

● c. 1410 Brunelleschi describes mathematical perspective

● 1525 The battle of Pavia

● 1427 Bruni becomes Chancellor of Florence

● 6-13 May 1527 The Sack of Rome

● 1434 The Medici family comes to power in Florence

● 1490 Collapse of the Medici banking business

● c. 1439 Gutenberg invents the printing press

● 1492 Columbus sails to America

1449-1515 Aldus Manutius, Venetian printer

● 31 October 1517 Luther's Ninety-five Theses

1499-1503 Cesare Borgia's campaigns in the Papal States

1452-1498 Girolamo Savonarola, revolutionary Florentine preacher

● 1453 Constantinople is captured by the Ottoman Turks

1454-1512 Amerigo Vespucci, explorer

1505-1508 Castiglione stays in Urbino

Famous People and Events

1460s First printing presses in Italy

● 1528 Castiglione's book *The Courtier* is published

● c. 1516 Machiavelli writes *The Prince*

c. 1462-1509 Caterina Sforza

1474-1539 Isabella d'Este

● c. 1550 Women are first allowed to perform on stage

1475-1497 Beatrice d'Este

● 1580 Palladio designs the fir permanent theatre

● 1501 Ottaviano Petrucci publishes printed music

● c. 1430 Donatello's *David*

1508-1512 Michelangelo paints the Sistine Chapel ceiling

1508-1514 Raphael paints the Stanza della Segnatura in the Vatican

● c. 1495 Leonardo paints *The Last Supper*

THE CLASSICAL RENAISSANCE   THE HIGH RENAISSANCE

Rulers

Popes

Pius II 1458-1464

Alexander VI 1492-1503

Leo X 1513-1521

Paul III 1534-1549

Nicholas V 1447-1455

Sixtus IV 1471-1484

Julius II 1503-1513

Clement VII 1523-1534

Mantua

Gianfrancesco Gonzaga 1407-1444   Lodovico Gonzaga 1444-1478   Francesco II Gonzaga 1484-1519

Rimini

Sigismondo Malatesta 1432-1468

Florence

Cosimo de' Medici 1434-1464   Lorenzo de' Medici, the Magnificent 1469-1492

Ferrara

Leonello d'Este 1441-1450   Ercole d'Este 1471-1505

Naples

Alfonso I 1442-1458   Ferrante I 1458-1494

Urbino

Federico da Montefeltro 1444-1482   Guidobaldo 1482-1508   Lorenzo de' Medici 1516-1519

Milan

Galeazzo Maria Sforza 1466-1476   Lodovico Sforza 1494-1500

France

Charles VIII 1483-1498   Francis I 1515-1547

Holy Roman Empire

Charles V 1519-1556

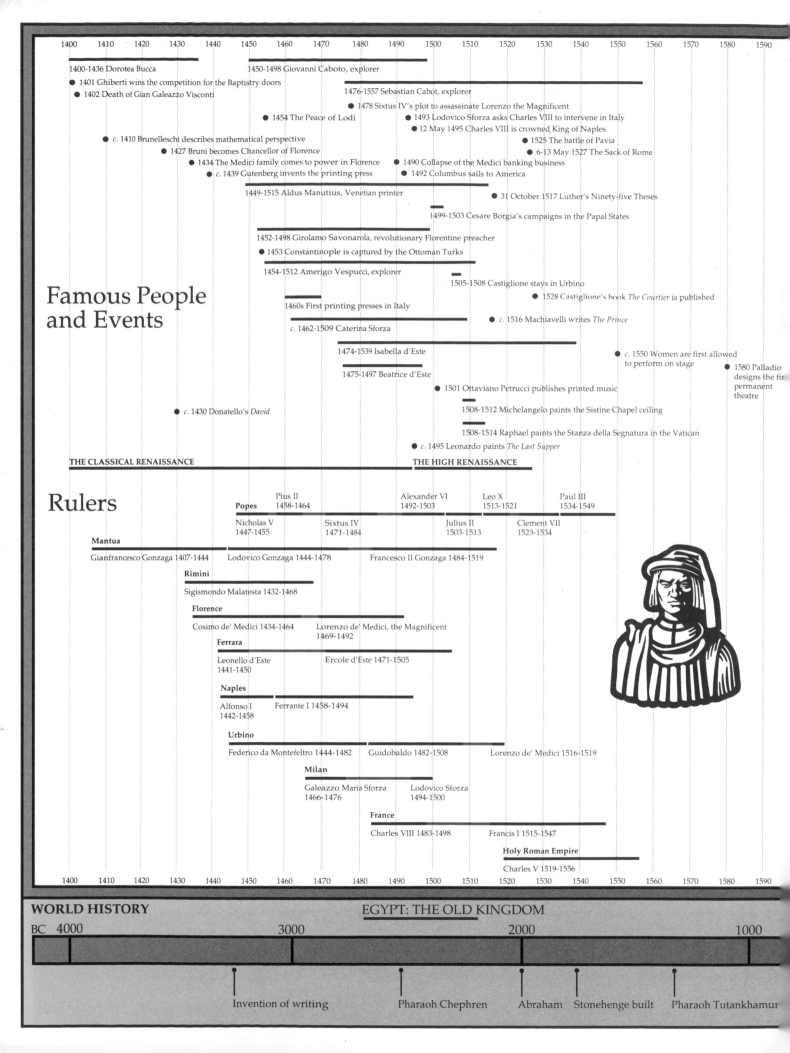

| 1400 | 1410 | 1420 | 1430 | 1440 | 1450 | 1460 | 1470 | 1480 | 1490 | 1500 | 1510 | 1520 | 1530 | 1540 | 1550 | 1560 | 1570 | 1580 | 1590 |

WORLD HISTORY   EGYPT: THE OLD KINGDOM

BC 4000   3000   2000   1000

Invention of writing   Pharaoh Chephren   Abraham   Stonehenge built   Pharaoh Tutankhamur